W9-AES-478

SHIPWRECKED!

The True Adventures of a Japanese Boy

RHODA BLUMBERG

HarperCollins*Publishers*

Also by RHODA BLUMBERG

Commodore Perry in the Land of the Shogun
Full Steam Ahead: The Race to Build a Transcontinental Railroad
The Incredible Journey of Lewis and Clark
The Great American Gold Rush
The Remarkable Voyages of Captain Cook
What's the Deal?: Jefferson, Napoleon, and the Louisiana Purchase

I am grateful for the brilliant guidance of my editor, Barbara Lalicki,
who always enhances the quality of my books.

Library of Congress Cataloging-in-Publication Data
Blumberg, Rhoda.
Shipwrecked!: the true adventures of a Japanese boy / Rhoda Blumberg.
p. cm.
Summary: In 1841, rescued by an American whaler after a terrible shipwreck leaves him and
his four companions castaways on a remote island, fourteen-year-old Manjiro learns new laws
and customs as he becomes the first Japanese person to set foot in the United States.
ISBN 0-688-17484-1 (trade)—ISBN 0-06-029365-9 (library)
1. Nakahama, Manjira, 1827–1898—Juvenile literature.
2. Japan—History—19th century—Juvenile literature.
3. Japan—Relations—United States—Juvenile literature.
4. United States—Relations—Japan—Juvenile literature.   I. Title.
DS881.5.N3 B58 2001   952'.025'092—dc21   [B]   99-86664

Typography by Stephanie Bart-Horvath
1 2 3 4 5 6 7 8 9 10
❖
First Edition

*T*itle page: Manjiro Nakahama photographed in his later years
Maps on pages 37 and 51 by Sergio Ruzzier

For Jerry and our crew of children and grandchildren

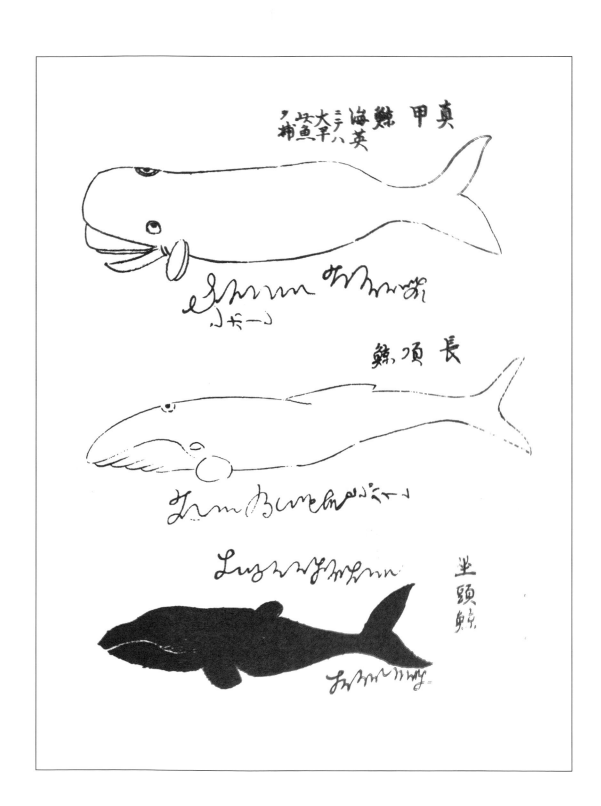

Sketches of whales by Manjiro

CONTENTS

A *Japanese fishing village, nestled close to shore*

SHIPWRECKED

HEAD OF THE FAMILY AT THE AGE OF NINE! When his father died in 1836, Manjiro had to support his mother, three younger sisters, one younger brother, and an invalid older brother who was too weak to work. Manjiro's family lived in poverty, as did their neighbors. Their squalid shacks were huddled together, hugging Japan's shore in Nakahama, a village in the province of Tosa. The men were fishermen, a vocation that *had* to be handed down father to son. Manjiro's father had been a fisherman; therefore, Manjiro would be a fisherman. Sons were forbidden to find any other field of employment. That had been the law of the land for hundreds of years.

Day after day, Manjiro set out to sea with boatloads of men. His job consisted of unhooking fish and emptying nets. Because he was a child, he had no chance to cast and catch. The men paid him by giving him fish to take home. They were very poor and could not afford to be more generous.

After five years of this child labor, Manjiro was unable to advance past the position of being a mere helper. And so he sought work at Usa, another coastal village ninety miles away. A fisherman called Denzo questioned him, and after learning about Manjiro's family's sad plight, Denzo welcomed him aboard a small fishing boat that he had borrowed from a friend. The crew consisted of

A *poor fisherman*

Denzo, his two brothers, Goemon and Jusuke, his friend Toraemon, and Manjiro.

The group loaded the boat with rice, firewood, and drinking water, preparing to spend up to three days at sea. On the morning of January 5, 1841, they rowed thirty miles out and cast all the nets they had, but there wasn't a fish to be caught. At night, they anchored near shore and slept fitfully until sunrise. The next day at sea proved equally disappointing, even when they tried their luck with rods and straw ropes strung with hooks. Again they lay at anchor for the night.

The third day, they ran into a school of mackerel. They were gleefully casting and filling their nets when the sky turned black. Before they could get ready to head in, walls of waves banged against their boat with such force that their oars and rudder were washed away. Then a ferocious wind attacked. It broke their mast and ripped their sail. The terrified crew expected to be dumped into the ocean. It was a miracle that the boat didn't capsize. Instead, it went on a wild ride, steered by wind and waves.

When night fell, sleet and freezing cold added to the group's agony. Their drenched clothes were frozen stiff. Icicles hung from their sleeves, sashes, and hair. Fortunately, the icicles, composed of freshwater, proved to be lifesavers. They sucked them, for their supply of drinking water had gone overboard. Sleet scraped from the boat also satisfied their thirst. And cold raw chunks of the mackerel they had caught halted their hunger.

Day after day, they clung to the sides of the boat, riding the swells of the sea, terrified, trembling from winter's cold, waiting for death to end their misery. At the mercy of water and wind, they helplessly rode the waves, not knowing when or where their lives would end.

The storm lasted one week without letup. On the eighth day, the ocean became calm, yet the disabled boat was carried forward by a strong underwater current. The fishermen felt as though they had fallen off the edge of the earth, for they could see nothing but sky and sea.

At noon, Denzo said he spotted an island floating on the horizon. Since the others didn't see it, they suspected that suffering had caused Denzo to hallucinate. But soon, land loomed ahead for everyone. They had sighted the island of Torishima, located more than three hundred miles from Japan. Using pieces of boards as oars, they rowed with all their might until the boat was about half a mile from shore. The island's steep cliffs looked forbidding. Rocks and reefs just above the water's surface kept them from rowing closer. They were all paralyzed with fear. How could they land without crashing their craft? Rather than risk immediate action, they delayed decision by spending the night on board their battered boat. At daylight, they rowed around the island, looking in vain for a safe place to land. Because the shallow waters were spiked with rocks, they could not row to shore. Therefore, they decided to swim.

They jumped into the sea just minutes before their boat crashed against sharp rocks and was smashed to bits. All swam for their lives. Fright, and the fight for survival, supplied their bodies with unusual energy. Exhausted, and freezing from cold, they helped one another climb ashore.

Jusuke was in dreadful shape. His leg had been badly hurt by their boat's floating debris. But, despite severe pain, he joined the others, climbing a cliff to level land. Then all of them collapsed, glad to be on solid ground.

無人島東面之図

船中ヨリ島ノ
大ニ峯ニ群飛ス
待ノ峯ハ其モレ
キハ站シ山形ヲ
共ノ事アリト云

「東面之図」
参考漂客伝」

The deserted island of Torishima, where Manjiro was shipwrecked.
The sketch is signed John Mung, the name Americans gave Manjiro.

MAROONED

MANJIRO AND DENZO WERE FIRST ON THEIR FEET. They told the others that they would explore the land and return with a report. Their findings were disheartening. The island was no more than two miles around, with steep slopes rising everywhere, directly from the sea. It was just a jumble of rocks and volcanic ash with a few scrubby, inedible plants and swarms of large white birds waddling about, clattering, whistling, and croaking.

The island of Torishima is the only breeding ground for colonies of short-tailed albatross. Thousands of these large, beautiful snow-white creatures nest on the island's cliffs, safe because there are no predators. The birds obtain all their food by flying and fishing in the ocean. Albatross don't need freshwater, because their bodies filter salt water into a nourishing liquid.

There were caves in this bird city. The largest they could find was just about big enough to shelter the group. The castaways made it their headquarters. The entrance was so small, they had to crouch to enter it. At home, all were accustomed to sleeping on the ground in their huts, where mats covered the dirt floors. Instead of mats, boards that had drifted ashore from their bashed boat were slid inside and laid on top of the ground. (The wood had no use as fuel because their flint for making fire had gone overboard.) Living conditions were

Trapped on an island of birds

miserable. Their shelter was cramped, dank, and dark. But it was better than being exposed to bad weather and living among noisy, beak-clicking birds.

The injured Jusuke wasn't able to fend for himself. His brother Denzo took care of him. As a result, the task of finding food belonged to the others. These exiled islanders survived by eating seaweed and a sparse supply of shellfish found clinging to rocks. They also gulped down the raw flesh of albatross. To vary their menu, Manjiro sometimes skinned albatross, then dried their meat in the sun. The birds had never encountered humans, or any other predators, and therefore were so tame and unafraid that they did not waddle away when anyone approached to grab them. They could fly only if they took off with a running start from a high cliff.

Freshwater trapped in the crevices of hollow rocks provided drinking water, but the supply was so limited that the unfortunate five agreed upon this rule: One oyster shell filled with water was allowed with each albatross eaten. They stored water in a pail that had been washed ashore from their wrecked boat.

After several weeks, Toraemon and Goemon became feverishly ill. Manjiro, the youngest and brightest of the group, was the only one able to leave the cave and bring back provisions.

The short-tailed albatross, which now breeds solely on Torishima

In April, the group survived an earthquake that nearly entombed them. The castaways had been resting inside their cave when they were jolted by tremors that made them quake in terror. They heard horrendous noises as rocks fell and showers of stones blocked the entrance to their cave. Fearing the cave could be their death trap, the castaways worked frantically, panting, straining, dripping with sweat, until they cleared the entrance and saw daylight.

In May, the albatross migrated. The group nearly starved.

The fishermen had been prisoners on an island for five months! During that time, the castaways endured bone-chilling cold, hunger, loneliness, and, worst of all, the outlook of hopelessness. They had no idea where on earth they were, but they did know they were far away from Japan, a country that had deliberately isolated itself from the rest of the world.

The Tokaido was Japan's longest, most important road. It skirted along between the hills and the coast from Kyoto, home of the emperor, to Edo, the capital city.

AN ISOLATED EMPIRE

THE GOVERNMENT OF JAPAN ENFORCED THOUSANDS OF LAWS to isolate its people from the rest of the world. Foreigners were not allowed in the land. Even books about foreigners were banned. In the 1830s, most Japanese people didn't know that the French Revolution, the American Revolution, and the Industrial Revolution had taken place. Anyone who left the Land of the Rising Sun gave up his right to return home, because he had been "poisoned" by outside influence and by forbidden information.

Many Japanese people were led to believe that other nations were evil empires made up of monsters. They had been taught that men and women who lived in other parts of the world were treacherous. Words like *barbarian, devil,* and *demon* were used to describe anyone from overseas. Only a few scholars had access to maps. But these maps were often mythological, not geographical, with sketches of misshapen beasts and frightening fiends who inhabited faraway lands. Japan was depicted as the heavenly blessed center of the universe.

Because people from other nations were looked upon as enemy aliens, foreign ships were prohibited in Japanese ports. Their captains and crew risked prison or death if they did not heed the closed-door policy of isolation.

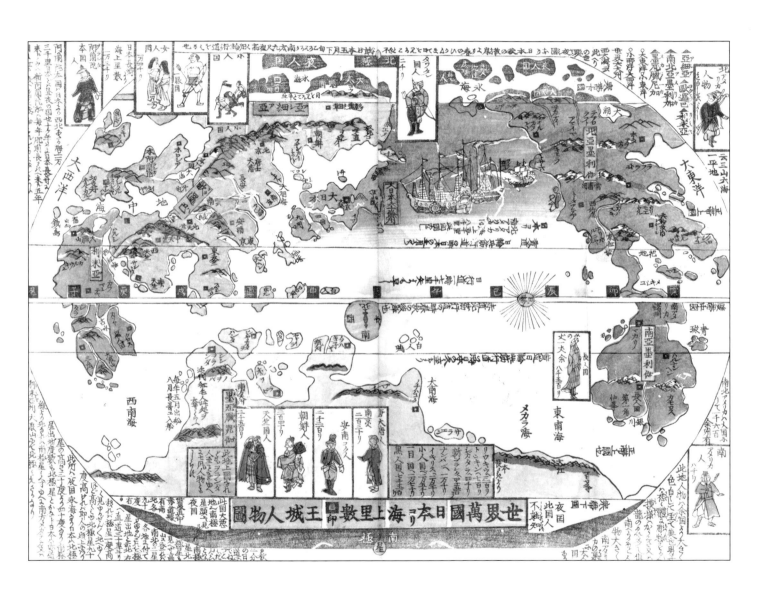

A wood-block-print map of the time shows Japan as one of the world's largest countries.

Dutchmen were the only foreign traders permitted in Japan at that time. These "barbarians" lived like prisoners, guarded by police, confined behind a high wall on the tiny island of Deshima, in Nagasaki harbor. They were there because of trade. They brought in firearms, fabrics, tobacco, and spectacles for the wealthy Japanese, and took out copper, gold, and silks for the European market. The Dutch traders also offered a window to the outside world for a select number of high-level Japanese officials and scholars by bringing them books and maps.

No more than twelve or thirteen Dutchmen took turns living there. They were not allowed to leave their island prison more than once or twice a year. Then they needed special permission from police, who accompanied them, monitored their actions and speech, and made sure that they did not talk to anyone except designated officials, who received very limited information about the world across the sea. Ships of other nations stayed away; it wasn't worth risking lives in order to visit or trade with a hostile country.

Japan would succeed in maintaining peace for nearly two and a half centuries (1603–1855)—a record never matched by any other nation. During this time, the nation prospered, flourishing in art and literature.

However, in this era, known as the Great Peace, people's freedom was limited by the enforcement of rigid rules and ruthless punishments. Laws specified every phase of people's existence:

- Where they lived. (People were not permitted to travel outside their home district unless they received permission from the police.)
- The size, design, and structure of their homes. (Wood huts and dirt or cobblestone floors were required for fishermen.)
- Whatever they owned. (Kinds of lanterns and types of toys were specified.)
- How they behaved. (The lower the bow, the more important the person being greeted. For nobility, one had to kowtow—get down on all fours, placing one's forehead on the ground.)
- The design of the clothing. (Regulations listed 216 varieties of dress for everyone

*K*omei, the emperor of Japan, 1831–1866, in imperial dress

from the emperor down to the lowest-class citizen. Even the material, the color of the garment, and the size and number of stitches were defined by edicts.)

Disobedience brought harsh penalties.

The stranded fishermen were sure they were doomed to live out the rest of their lives on this bleak island. They dreamed of going home but realized that even if, by chance, some ship were to rescue them and take them back to Japan, they would be convicted by this law:

■ Any person who leaves the country to go to another and later returns will be put to death.

The reality of rescue was far-fetched. The following laws made sure that no Japanese ship would be able to sail as far as their boat had drifted:

■ The sending of ships to any foreign country is forbidden.
■ The construction of large ships [capable of sailing long distances] is prohibited.

People were limited to small boats that could be used for fishing or transporting merchandise along Japan's coast and among its islands. Fishermen and cargo boatmen were given some leeway: They were allowed to be away for several days. But weeks and months! No excuse was acceptable—not even shipwreck. Anyone who disobeyed edicts that specified limited travel risked imprisonment or a death sentence.

Here they were, far away from home, forsaken! They would have to spend the rest of their lives marooned on this miserable island.

Flagging down the ship

RESCUED

ONE JUNE MORNING, WHILE GATHERING SHELLFISH on the shore and gazing at the endless sea, Manjiro was fascinated by a black dot on the watery horizon. The dot grew bigger and bigger as it came near. It was a ship, a huge one, larger than any ship Manjiro had ever seen.

He raced back to the cave to get the others. The crippled Jusuke waited impatiently with his brother Denzo, as his other brother, Goemon, and their friend Toraemon rushed to the shore for the incredible sight. Toraemon picked up a plank that waves had thrown on the shore, tied a piece of his own tattered clothing to it, and waved it frantically, hoping to attract the attention of someone on the oncoming ship.

The giant vessel folded its sails, approached their island, dropped anchor, then lowered two bulky boats into the water. The boats, each carrying six men, headed toward shore—but not toward the castaways! The strangers were heading for another part of the island. The marooned men panicked because they weren't noticed. Little did they know that these boats had been launched with orders to search for turtles. (Turtles were ideal for a ship's larder because they could be stored alive for months without being fed, and their meat was delicious.)

Small boats were sent out from the big ship for whale hunts and to find food.

Luckily, just as they were about to row around a bend, the turtle hunters sighted Manjiro and his group. They shouted something in a language that the castaways could not understand. Then one of the boatmen motioned to them, using gestures of pantomime. Manjiro guessed that they were being told to swim to these men. He waded into the water, dove under a high wave, and, with steady strokes, swam to one of the boats. Goemon and Toraemon followed him. Strong arms pulled them on board.

When they looked at their rescuers, the castaways became fearful. The foreigners' features were completely different from any they had ever seen before. They never dreamed that men with such long noses, hairy faces, light eyes, and light hair inhabited earth. And, oh, the weird clothing! Leather boots instead of straw sandals, narrow-sleeved shirts, and body-clinging pants instead of kimonos! However, even though the foreigners looked strange, there was no choice but to trust them, especially because these "barbarians" acted with kindness and concern.

Using the common language of gesture, Manjiro pointed to the island, and indicated that others were stranded there. Because rocks and reefs made dock-

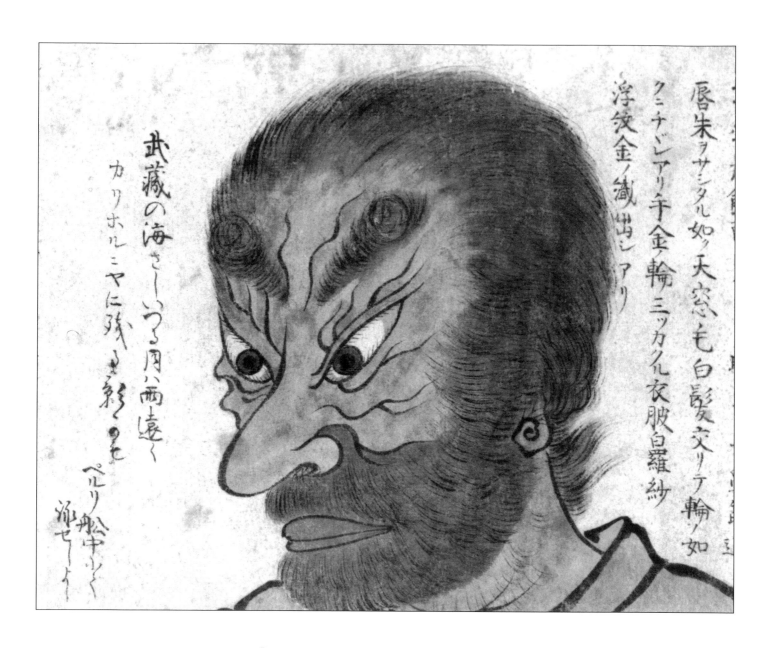

A Japanese artist's view of a foreigner

ing on the island dangerous, two of the boatmen swam to shore with Manjiro. When they entered the cave, Jusuke and Denzo were so frightened, they shrank back in terror. Manjiro calmed them down and explained that these odd-looking aliens came from a ship that would sail them away from their island prison. Denzo carried his crippled brother to shore; then, clutching him, swam with the others to one of the boats.

*T*he John Howland, *with its sails down*

THE WHALING SHIP

THE CAPTAIN OF THE SHIP MADE THIS ENTRY IN HIS LOGBOOK, Sunday, June 27,1841: "Sent two boats to see if there was any turtle, found 5 poor distressed people on the isle, took them off, could not understand anything from them more than they were hungry."

After boarding the boat, the five castaways were rowed to the most enormous ship they had ever seen in their lives. It was 180 feet from bow to stern, 36 feet wide, with three masts 100 feet high, flying white sails. It was so big that, in addition to the two boats used by the turtle hunters, there were four more boats lashed to its sides.

The group had been rescued by the seamen of an American whaler, the *John Howland*. The ship had set out from the port of New Bedford, Massachusetts, and had been at sea hunting whales for twenty months. The crew of thirty-four men was under the command of Captain William H. Whitfield. Only thirty-six years old, he was nevertheless a seasoned old salt who had been chasing ocean prey for more than twenty years. Whitfield was highly respected, especially because—unlike other captains of that time—he did not believe in flogging. Instead, anyone who disobeyed orders was punished by having privileges taken away, or by having money deducted from his share of the profits.

Captain William H. Whitfield

The captain ordered his men to provide clothing so that the castaways could change from their wet rags. For the first time in their lives, the rescued five wore shirts and pants with buttons and pockets. Buttons were unknown in Japan, where cords, strings, and sashes were used to fasten loose-fitting clothing. Pockets were also new to them. People at home carried small packages in their sleeves, tucked in sashes, or placed in the bosom of a kimono. The group was also surprised to see leather boots. In Japan, using leather, or any animal products, was against the law.

Before bedding down on a floor below deck, they were served a supper. In addition to soup, they ate bread, a food they had never eaten before.

At first, they were given their meals and confined below so that they would not interfere with the work of sailing and whaling. Although unable to understand the sailors' language, they easily interpreted their friendly attitudes and were very happy when, after some days, the captain allowed them to explore the ship.

They were amazed to find a food supply of live chickens and pigs. Spare provisions, sails, ropes, harpoons, and hundreds of casks containing whale oil were also stored below. The oil represented the captain's and crew's earnings from whale hunts. Instead of wages, each hand received a percentage of the profits, known as a lay. The size of the lay depended on the importance of a man's job. Ordinary

*T*he famous American author Herman Melville went whaling at the same time as Manjiro. This painting by Ambroise Louis Gargeray was greatly admired for its accuracy by Melville.

hands could be rewarded with as little as the 275th part of the prof-its of a voyage; skilled workers received more. The captain, the ship's owners, and the people in the United States who had financed the voyage made the most money. If the whale hunt was successful, everybody got paid. If it was not, nobody made a penny.

Herman Melville, the great American author, worked on a whaler in the Pacific Ocean in 1841, the very same year Manjiro and his group were on the *John Howland*. In *Moby-Dick*, Melville detailed what life was like on a typical whaler at that time, reporting that "of the grand order of folio leviathans, the Sperm Whale and the Right Whale are by far the most noteworthy. They are the only whales regularly hunted by man."

*P*eeling blubber
off the whale

Manjiro knew that whales were caught in Japan by coastal villagers far from his home. Their hunting methods were very different from those on the *John Howland*. They worked from land, with sentinels sighting their prey from hills overlooking the ocean. When a whale swam close to the shore, hundreds of people went into action. At least thirty longboats, each rowed by thirty to forty men, held enormous nets that were dropped overboard to encircle and trap a whale. After being blocked by nets, the whale was killed by harpooners. Then some men climbed onto the beast's back and others swam underneath to attach ropes from the monster to two boats that dragged it to shore. On the beach, the beast was butchered, packaged, and sold as food. Blubber, bones, and oil were often discarded. A killed whale was butchered for its value as food. The best cuts were set aside for the tables of nobility.

Until a whale was caught, Manjiro and his friends could not understand why there were two enormous brick ovens dominating the top deck. These were try ovens for cooking chunks of blubber (whale fat), which, when boiled, turned into oil. The carcass of one whale could hold tons of valuable oil. In those days, before oil wells were drilled, whale oil was used to light lamps, lubricate machinery, and make items such as soaps, perfumes, candles, and medicine. The Japanese did not know about the many uses of oil at that time.

Cooking the blubber to make oil

Sperm whales' jaws, which could measure twenty feet in length, were hoisted on deck. The teeth were dug out with sharp spades, then stored, to be sold later as precious ivory. Melville reported that the sea beasts' bones were "sawn into slabs and piled away like joists for building houses." These were made into gateposts, rafters, and fences and were also fashioned into furniture.

The heads of right whales were often hoisted on board, too. When pried open, the insides of their jaws could measure twenty feet long, five feet high, and twelve feet wide—a cave roomy enough for several men to enter. A right whale's toothless mouth was filled with unique treasures. Melville wrote that "the lower lip . . . will yield you some 500 gallons of oil, and more." The hundreds of boards of baleen that curtain the whale's upper jaw to strain its food were used for making items such as buggy whips, carriage springs, canes, fishing rods, umbrella ribs, rakes, and stiffeners for women's corsets and hoops for their skirts. Whaling was a mammoth, highly profitable business for nineteenth-century New Englanders.

Between hunts, the crew kept busy swabbing decks, constructing casks, repairing ropes, fixing sails—keeping things shipshape. There was always a lookout perched one hundred feet above deck at the top of the main mast, spyglass in hand, watching for whales.

Manjiro amazed everyone, from captain to cabin boy, because after a few weeks he learned to speak and understand English. He asked for the chance to climb the ropes to the top of the main mast and stand watch as lookout.

His very first time at this job, Manjiro spied a spout, the fountain of vapor made by the breath of a whale surfacing for air. He shouted the traditional "There she blows . . . blows!"—a call that brought quick action. Four boats were lowered, each with one harpooner, one skipper, and four rowers. They surrounded the ocean giant, then gave chase as their prey sounded by diving deep underwater. It could be an hour and a half before the whale came up to get its needed breath of air. Then the boats closed in. Harpooners hurled their

Standing watch at the top of the main mast

weapons until the sea around them streaked red with blood. Secured with ropes, a wounded whale often pulled a boat for many miles before it collapsed and died.

Ropes on the boats were used to drag and fasten the dead whale to the ship's starboard side. One man stood on top of the whale to attach a chain with a huge hook to its back. Then the carcass was cut into slabs by men who worked from the main deck with twenty-foot-long razor-sharp spades. Using block and tackle, the blubber was lifted on board, where it was cut up into smaller chunks and boiled in huge try-pots.

The entire process fascinated Manjiro and his group, who had never caught anything larger than a sea bass. They admired experienced whale hunters who risked their lives fighting sea monsters. Not only was the boat's crew in danger when a whale was harpooned, but the *John Howland* was also in peril. Ships had been wrecked by infuriated whales. There was hardly a harpooner who hadn't heard about the awful fate of the Nantucket ship the *Essex*. In 1819, it sank to the bottom of the Pacific after a headstrong whale rammed a huge hole in the ship's side with its head. (Luckily, the crew had enough time to escape in their whaleboats.)

Manjiro was particularly interested in learning the skills needed to navigate a big ship. Captain Whitfield was so enchanted by the boy's brilliance and passion for learning that he taught him to read maps and lectured him on the art of piloting. At times, he handed over the helm to allow Manjiro the thrill of steering the ship. This was exciting for Manjiro, and diverting, because his heart ached. Leisure time was agony because he worried about his family, and he despaired that he would never see them again.

Captain Whitfield gave the boy a name easier for Americans to pronounce than Manjiro. Everyone called him John Mung.

Manjiro drew this picture.

Hawaii, the Pacific Ocean's port of call for whale ships and merchant ships

HONOLULU

THE SHIP CONTINUED TO HUNT IN THE WHALE-RICH WATERS near Japan, but it never sailed close to the shore. Captain Whitfield feared the Japanese might open fire and attack the *John Howland* as they had done in 1837 when the American ship *Morrison* sailed into Edo (Tokyo) Bay. He could not risk having his ship destroyed and his men killed or captured. The situation dismayed Manjiro, who wanted to return home. He would willingly have risked his own life to get back to his family, for he feared that they might be suffering because he could not provide for them. But he realized the captain could not jeopardize the safety of the *John Howland* and its crew.

After catching nineteen whales, the captain headed his ship for the Sandwich Islands (Hawaii) for supplies and provisions. When the ship docked at Honolulu's harbor, the island newspaper, *The Polynesian,* announced, "ARRIVED: November 20, 1841. *John Howland,* New Bedford, 24 mons [months at sea, carrying] 1400 sperm [barrels of sperm-whale oil]."

The Honolulu of 1841 was a forest of masts, crowded with New England whaling ships and merchant ships from the United States, France, and England. Manjiro and his group were elated, for they had never been to a busy harbor.

The castaways were thrilled to disembark and walk along roads lined with shops and taverns. They saw houses whose structures were new to them. There

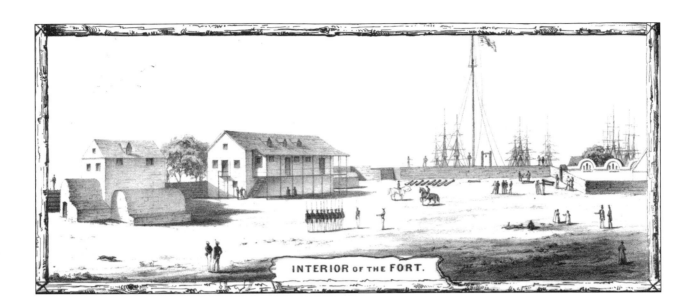

INTERIOR of the FORT.

Manjiro and his friends lived at this fort for a short time.

were the thatched huts of Hawaiians and the wooden houses of Americans. The framed New England–style wooden homes were occupied by sea captains' families, by merchants who had established shops near the docks, and by American missionaries who were converting many Hawaiians to Christianity.

Captain Whitfield took the castaways to the home of Dr. Gerrit P. Judd, an American medical missionary who wielded political power. Dr. Judd had renounced his American citizenship to swear allegiance to the king of Hawaii. As a result, His Royal Highness Kamehameha III appointed Judd as his most powerful personal adviser. This missionary acted as governor of the islands. (In 1842, he was named prime minister.) He made arrangements for the Japanese group to live first at a fort, then at a home in Honolulu. He told them that all their expenses would be paid by the government.

Although Denzo, Goemon, Jusuke, and Toraemon chose to remain in Hawaii, where Dr. Judd assured them comfort and the chance to find jobs, Manjiro decided to stay with the ship. Since he could not return to his homeland, he desperately wished to shape his life under the captain's guidance. He wanted to become a qualified navigator. Captain Whitfield, who was a childless widower at this time, ached to act as this remarkable boy's foster parent. He was elated at the prospect of having Manjiro return home with him.

After arranging for the whale oil to be transferred to other ships so that it could be taken to ports in the United States and having stocked the *John Howland* with hogs, fresh fruit, and water, Captain Whitfield ordered his ship to set sail in January 1842. Manjiro became a member of the crew. He was to receive 1/140th of the profits as his share. He was sixteen years old.

The men spent sixteen months on the Pacific Ocean hunting whales; then, after a stopover at the island of Guam for supplies, rounding Cape Horn, and sailing among icebergs, they went up along the east coasts of the Americas. On May 7, 1843, they arrived at New Bedford, Massachusetts. The *John Howland* had been away from its home port for three years and seven months. Manjiro had been away from his homeland for two and a half years.

By bringing Manjiro, Captain Whitfield introduced Americans to a boy who had come from the locked-up land of mystery—the isolated empire of Japan. Manjiro was to be baffled by the strangeness of an alien world—the United States.

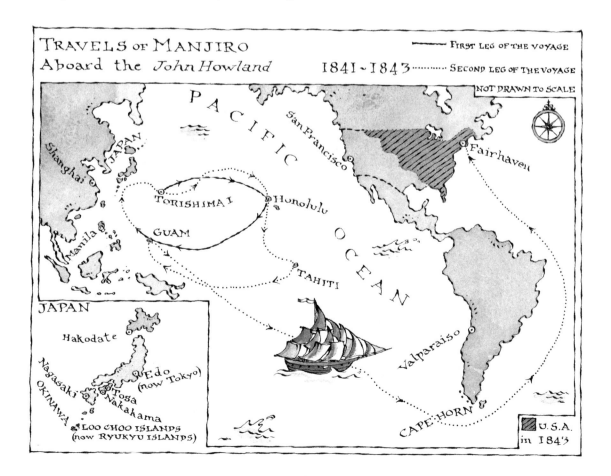

*T*he John Howland *in full sail*

A JAPANESE
NEW ENGLANDER

MANJIRO WAS THE FIRST JAPANESE PERSON to set foot in the United States. After disembarking, Captain Whitfield took Manjiro to the Seaman's Bethel Church to offer prayers of thanks for their safe, successful voyage. Then he took the boy across the first drawbridge Manjiro had ever seen in his life. It spanned the Acushnet River, connecting New Bedford with the small town of Fairhaven on the opposite side of the harbor.

They headed for the home of Eben Akin, a former officer on one of Whitfield's whalers. Because the captain had to leave for New York City to find buyers for oil and bones, he asked Akin to provide a temporary home for Manjiro. Akin was keen about keeping this foreign boy, and so arrangements were made. Whitfield not only paid for board, but also arranged for Akin to enroll the boy at the town's Stone School House on Bread and Cheese Lane.

Manjiro, at the age of sixteen, had never attended school in his life! He would begin his formal education in a one-room schoolhouse, among thirty children who ranged in age from four to sixteen. Until his body became accustomed to a sitting position, Manjiro found being seated on a bench behind a desk very uncomfortable. In Japan, people kneeled on the floor and sat back on their heels. Chairs and benches were not used.

As a unique alien, Manjiro was a curiosity to many folks. However, their interest in him did not compare to the enchantment he experienced when he saw the strange sights surrounding him. He was truly in a new world. Never before had he seen magnificent mansions, glorious gardens, and sky-high church steeples. The elegant section of the town, where families made rich from whale oil lived, was high on a hill above the wharves. Men in high silk hats and long-tailed coats walked alongside women in bonnets and long, tight-waisted gowns. (Manjiro had become familiar with Western dress when he was in Hawaii, but he never had seen clothes as elaborate and elegant as those worn by well-to-do New Englanders.) At times, a gentleman held a woman's arm as he helped her across a road. (In Japan, women did not walk with men; they followed behind them, and touching the arm of a female in public was considered crude.)

Inspecting barrels of whale oil on the New Bedford docks

Close to the waterfront, there were warehouses for whale products, stores for butchers, bakers, and candle makers, and shops for

harpoons, hardwood, hammocks, and a thousand other things. Oil barrels were piled high on the wharves. They also lined the long lanes. Author-whaler Herman Melville had lived in New Bedford. He wrote that "the town itself is a land of oil . . . [where] . . . fathers they say, give whales for dowers to their daughters." Whale oil was used as currency. Teachers and ministers were sometimes paid with barrels of oil instead of cash. Although the stench of whale oil was offensive to some outsiders, to those who lived there the smell was perfume that enhanced the well-being of the whole town. New Bedford at that time was the greatest whaling port in the world.

Taverns and boardinghouses were filled with young men and old salts from all over the world. Streets swarmed with seamen from the islands of the Pacific, as well as those from Africa and Europe. Local country boys yearning to go to sea intermingled with them. The young American hayseeds listened eagerly to mariners' tales about the allure of faraway islands, the challenge of fighting sea monsters, the spell of the sea. Rarely did they want to hear about the hard work, poor food, and the desperately lonely life aboard a ship that wouldn't return to home port for three or four years.

Captain Whitfield's business trip lasted two months. During that time, he had courted and married Albertina Keith, an attractive, gentle woman. The captain built a house outside of Fairhaven and started a farm. Manjiro was thrilled to move in with the newlyweds. The house had unique features not found in Japan:

Glass windows—not translucent paper windows
Separate rooms for sleeping, eating, lounging—not one all-purpose room
Solid interior walls—not sliding screens made of paper
Chairs—not found in Japanese homes, where people sat on the floor
Beds—not straw mats on the floor
Pillows—not a bag of grain or a log for a headrest
Whale-oil candles—not candles made from the resin of a pine tree
Tin and glass lanterns—not paper or wood lanterns

Manjiro was amazed that Captain Whitfield owned fourteen acres of land. In Japan, only noblemen controlled more than a small plot of ground. Manjiro enjoyed farming—an occupation forbidden to him in Japan. And he loved riding horseback—an activity denied to anyone in his country who was not a samurai or a daimyo (lord). After school and during the summers, he harvested vegetables and tended horses. He noted that neighboring farmers raised cattle for milk and beef. In Japan, cattle were not milked or butchered. The thought of drinking something produced by animals seemed unclean, and eating beef was against the law in his country. There, cattle were used for pulling carts and carrying loads.

Manjiro was a pupil at the Stone School House.

The Whitfields loved Manjiro as their own son. How proud they were to learn that their boy was a brilliant student ready for more advanced studies! They enrolled him at Bartlett's Academy, a school in Fairhaven that gave courses in navigation and surveying. The

curriculum was geared to train future mariners who might become ships' officers and captains.

Although some looked askance at a foreign face that seemed out of place in a school that catered to sons of New England shipmasters and shipowners, others respected Manjiro for his superior mind and winning personality. He was the brightest student in the class. A friend described him as "shy and quiet in his demeanor," adding that John Mung "fairly soaked up learning."

After two and a half years at Bartlett's, Manjiro decided he was old enough to earn his own keep. He became a live-in apprentice for Mr. William Hussey, a gruff character who made casks for keeping oil. Manjiro was overworked and underfed by William Hussey. After six months, he became so ill that he had to move back to the Whitfield farm, where the concerned captain and his wife nursed him back to health.

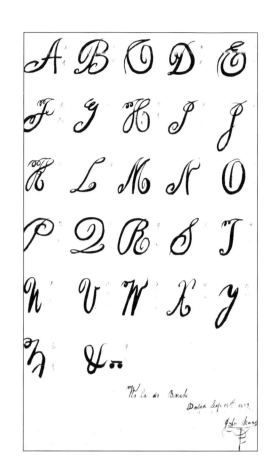

*T*he alphabet, written by Manjiro

Although grateful and loving toward the Whitfields, Manjiro longed for the affection, attention, and approval of his mother, and he often thought about his life in Japan. He dreamed of returning to his homeland and telling his family about some of the strange customs of Americans. He wrote the following comments:

- "When a young man wants to marry, he looks for a young woman for himself without asking a go-between to find one for him, as we do in Japan."
- "American men and women make love openly. [They kiss in public.]"
- "Women do not use paint or powder on their faces."
- "American women have quaint customs. For instance, some of

ヌーバッホー港頭之畐

A Japanese illustrator who was guided by Manjiro's descriptions
drew this picture of Fairhaven.

them make a hole through the lobes of their ears and run a gold or silver ring through this hole as an ornament."

- "A mother . . . gives of all things, cow's milk as a substitute for mother's milk. But it is true that no ill effects of this strange habit have been reported."
- "Eggs, oil and salt mixed with flour is good food. They call it bread."
- "A man takes off his hat when paying a visit. [He does not remove his shoes.]"
- "A man and his host shake hands to greet each other. He never bows."
- "A man sits on a chair instead of the floor."
- "Ordinary men carry watches."
- "When walking they carry canes inside of which swords are often hidden."
- "Houses have glass windows [instead of oiled translucent paper], and woolen carpets [instead of straw mats] which are woven by machines."
- "Officials are hard to distinguish as they never display the authority of their office. [They don't dress distinctively to show their superior power. No one has to bow to them.]"

As an adopted member of a family, he reflected his feelings by writing, "Families are peaceful and affectionate. The happiness of their homes is not matched in other countries."

View of New Bedford, Massachusetts

A CRAZED CAPTAIN

IT WAS 1846—THE PEAK YEAR FOR AMERICAN WHALING. There was such a demand for experienced hands that ship captains had a hard time finding qualified men. Captain Ira Davis of the whaler *Franklin* found the task especially difficult because he ran a "religious ship" that observed the Sabbath and forbade grog, the liquor that kept most whalers in high spirits. Everyone hired had to sign Whaleman's Shipping Paper, which included the following clauses.

For officers:

NO DISTILLED SPIRITOUS LIQUOR WILL BE PUT ON BOARD. . . . In case of violation of this pledge by the Master or any Officer of Seamen, his entire share of the voyage shall be thereupon forfeited.

For the crew:

It shall be the duty of the Officer having care of the Log Book, to note . . . all instances of drunkenness . . . [and] . . . every instruct of women put into the ship for [immoral] licentious purposes. . . . For every instance of drunkenness two days' pay shall be forfeited.

The sketch shows Goemon (lower left) and Denzo (lower right).

what he was supposed to do. He physically attacked others for no apparent reason and shouted crazy commands. At first, the crew didn't speak out, for they were afraid of being accused of mutiny. But the captain became so violent and irrational that the crew concluded he was insane. Even though they risked being tried and sentenced to death for mutiny, they unanimously decided to remove the captain, put him in irons, and keep him shackled until they reached port. Based on votes from the crew, the first mate was elected captain. Manjiro, the cook's helper, was hailed as most qualified to be second in command because of his experience and training. He was unanimously chosen to be first mate.

Everyone was relieved when the ship docked at Manila, in the Philippines, and no one was accused of mutiny. An American consul confirmed that Captain Davis was too crazed to command a ship. The captain was forced to stay imprisoned in Manila until a ship could transfer him to the United States.

On September 23, 1849, after three years and four months at sea, and having had five hundred successful whale hunts, the *Franklin* returned to its home port of New Bedford. Manjiro had earned $350 as his share—more money than he had ever had in his life.

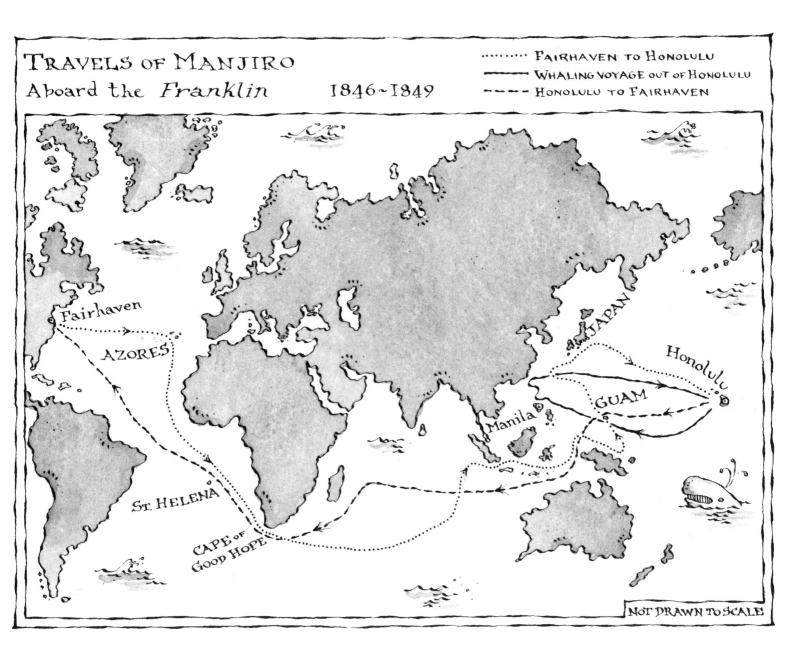

TRAVELS of MANJIRO
Aboard the *Franklin*   1846~1849

.... FAIRHAVEN to HONOLULU
———— WHALING VOYAGE out of HONOLULU
– – – HONOLULU to FAIRHAVEN

Fairhaven

AZORES

St. HELENA

CAPE of
GOOD HOPE

JAPAN

Honolulu

GUAM

Manila

NOT DRAWN TO SCALE

California News, a well-known painting by William Sidney Mount

DIGGING FOR GOLD

MANJIRO'S LIFE, LIKE THOUSANDS OF OTHERS, was changed by the discovery of gold in California in 1848. It was impossible to stay calm when one newspaper wrote about men opening up a vein of gold "just as coolly as you would a potato hill," and another stated that in California "gold is unbroken and extends over a tract of 120 miles in length and 70 miles in breadth." The most astounding report came from James Polk, the president of the United States, who announced to Congress, "The accounts of the abundance of gold . . . are of such extraordinary character as would scarcely command belief. . . . The supply is very large." The result was a raging epidemic of "gold fever." Wealth seemed guaranteed. People quit their jobs, left their homes, and headed for the hills of California.

Most gold seekers dreamed about hitting pay dirt and living in luxury for the rest of their lives. Manjiro dreamed of digging enough treasure to finance his return to Japan. He was tormented by a vision of his mother begging for food. He had not seen her for nearly ten years. Although aware that he could be imprisoned and killed for the sin of visiting a foreign country, he would risk death for peace of mind. He would stake his life to fulfill his duty as a son.

Upon receiving Captain Whitfield's approval, Manjiro found passage on the *Stieglitz,* a lumber ship that was to deliver its cargo on the West Coast. Even though he worked for no wages as a member of the crew, he had to pay twenty-five dollars for his passage. The vessel bucked ferocious storms to round Cape Horn, that "graveyard of ships." After stopping at Valparaiso, Chile, to take on fresh food and water, then sailing up the West Coast, the ship docked in San Francisco. The port was crammed with hundreds of unmanned ships that had been abandoned by crews who had deserted to head for the goldfields.

Manjiro was shocked by conditions in San Francisco, a town of tents and shanties. Muddy streets were strewn with garbage. The cheapest room he found—twenty dollars a week —was in a filthy shack. Inflation was so sky-high that onions, potatoes, and eggs

The boom town of San Francisco

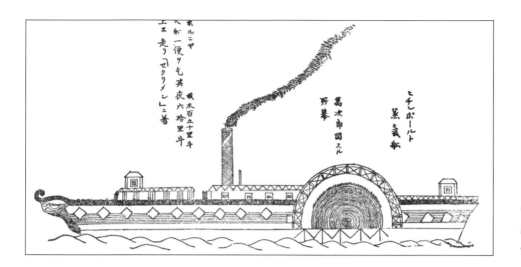

This sketch of a steamboat has been attributed to Manjiro.

cost one dollar each. Gambling houses and drinking saloons were everywhere. Crowds were raucous, and crime was rampant.

Everyone he met warned Manjiro to be on guard against robbers, and urged him to head for the hills as fast as he could. After a three-day stay in San Francisco, he traveled to Sacramento on a riverboat, which looked strange to him, for it had no masts or sails. A huge furnace on board boiled water and made steam. The force of the steam moved the boat by propelling an iron wheel fixed to it. Being a passenger on a steamboat was a new and exciting experience for Manjiro.

As soon as he reached Sacramento, he left town and hiked through steep mountain passes until he came to a gold mine where a company agent offered him work. Manjiro was paid six dollars a day for digging in a dark, dank hole in the ground. After a month, he quit to try his luck as an independent treasure hunter.

Manjiro found a shack whose owner charged two dollars a day for sleeping space on the floor. After spending two months panning for gold on the banks of a mountain stream, he washed up $600 worth of nuggets—enough to help finance his plans to return to Japan. He carried his sack of gold to a San Francisco bank, where he exchanged his precious metal for cash, then bought passage on the

*D*igging for gold

Eliza Warwick, a merchant steamship bound for Honolulu. Manjiro hoped it would be a mere stopover on the way to his native land.

On October 10, 1850, the *Eliza Warwick* steamed into Honolulu's harbor. Manjiro immediately visited his friends Denzo, Toraemon, and Goemon. He asked if they wanted to go to Japan with him. Toraemon refused to consider leaving. He declared that returning home was too risky. True stories had trickled into Hawaii by way of Dutch traders, who reported that foreigners who had been shipwrecked on Japanese shores had been shackled and locked in small cages. Denzo and Goemon, however, had been so unhappy and homesick that they were eager to go.

The Friend, a Honolulu newspaper, published the story of the castaways, with an appeal for funds and equipment. "To complete the outfit of the men is wanted . . . a compass, a good fowling piece, a few articles of clothing, shoes, and a nautical almanac for 1850."

The Hawaiians were happy to help, and, in addition to clothing, they contributed $160 in cash. Adding these funds to the money he had already set aside, Manjiro bought an old but sturdy whaleboat, which he hoped would be launched from a ship willing to anchor a safe distance from Japan's shores. He named his boat *Adventurer.* Manjiro bought gifts for his family: needles, scissors, buttons, medicines, a mirror, coffee, and white sugar—items not found in Japan. And he packed maps, books, including *A Life of George Washington,* an American atlas, and an almanac.

On December 17, 1850, the merchant ship *Sarah Boyd* docked in Honolulu. It was on the way to Shanghai, China, to take on teas and silks for the U.S. market. Manjiro immediately went to see the master of the ship, Captain Jacob Whitmore, and told him that he was one of three men who wanted to return to their homeland. He promised that he and his friends would work for no pay if they could be dropped off in Japanese waters, and that the ship could anchor a safe distance away from Japan to avoid being attacked and captured. Manjiro's boat, the *Adventurer,* would be lowered from deck, and then the three would row to shore.

The captain agreed to Manjiro's request because he was short of hands. Even in Honolulu, people had caught gold fever. Members of Whitmore's crew had deserted to board ships bound for California. Even though the captain didn't like sailing in enemy waters, he agreed to take Manjiro, Denzo, and Goemon near islands that were not far from Japan. The trio would then row to Japan on the *Adventurer.*

Manjiro carried a letter from the United States consul in Honolulu. It included the following statement: "I trust [these exiles] . . . may be kindly treated by all persons whom they meet. . . . Manjiro has sustained a good character and has improved in knowledge. He will tell his countrymen of Japan how happy the Americans would be to make their acquaintance, and visit them with their ships, and give gold and silver for their goods."

The departure of the *Sarah Boyd* with Manjiro, Denzo, and Goemon on board caused a stir of excitement in Hawaii. *The Friend* expressed the hopes of its readers: "We shall anxiously wait to learn the success of Captain Mung's expedition. Success to John Mung commanding the *Adventurer.*"

*L*ord Nariakira, the daimyo who protected Manjiro

ARRESTED

AFTER SAILING FOR SEVENTY DAYS, the *Sarah Boyd* stopped four miles from Okinawa, the largest of the Loo Choo Islands (the Ryukyu Islands). The ship did not have to change its course, for it passed by Okinawa on its way to Shanghai. Despite hail, sleet, and rough waters, Manjiro insisted that the *Adventurer* be lowered into the sea. He and his two friends climbed down into the bobbing craft. Waves that kept swamping the boat were as scary as those that had smashed their fishing boat to bits near the island of Torishima. Using superstrength that can come about in times of crisis, they rowed to shore.

When they landed, people who were on the beach fled in terror. They feared strangers not only because they knew nothing about them but also because their laws forbade contact with foreigners.

When the three newcomers walked to a cluster of houses a short distance from shore, adults grabbed their children, ran into their homes, and slammed their doors shut. Hoping for help, Manjiro called out to them in Japanese, but no one answered him. After a distressingly long time—perhaps only thirty minutes, but it felt like hours—a group of officials confronted Manjiro, Denzo, and Goemon and arrested them. They were locked up in a house surrounded by

- *"The American government is said to be the best in the world."*
- *"The character of the people is very generous and honest and they do little wrong."*
- *"America is working to develop its own country and has no time to attack other countries."*
- *"There is no hereditary king in this country. A man of great knowledge and ability is elected king. He sits on the throne for four years."*
- *"There is no distinction between classes. Even a man of low rank may become an official."*
- *"The present king is called Taylor. He lives very simply and goes about on horseback, followed by a single retainer."*
- *"The Americans are better tempered than the Japanese."*

This picture of a railroad train was drawn by an artist guided by Manjiro.

There were descriptions of a railroad, "an invention which runs on the land . . . 23 or four iron boxes chained together, on top of which the cargo is placed and within which passengers sit." Manjiro also talked about the amazing telegraph, which "uses a wire stretched high above the road and the letter hung on it goes from

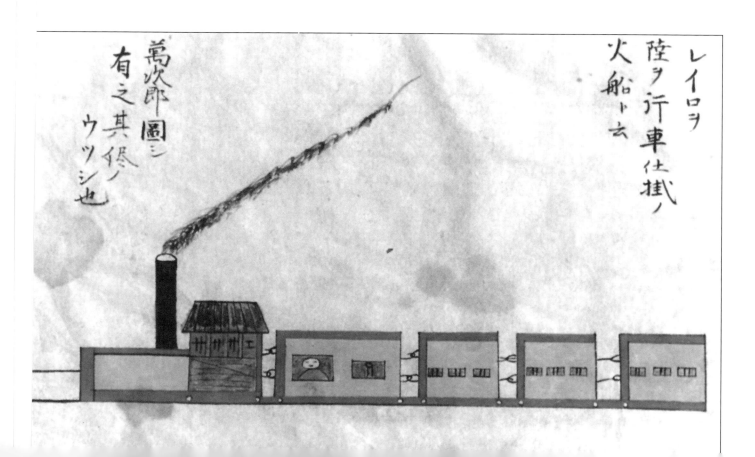

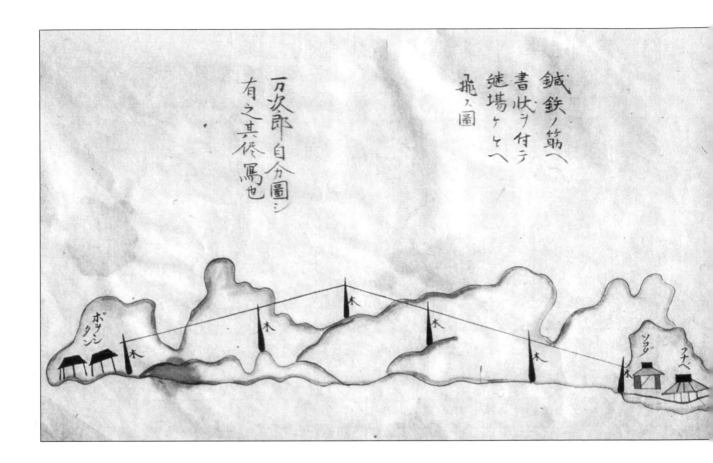

一万次郎自分圖シ
有之其侭寫也

鍼鉄ノ筋ヘ
書状ヲ付テ
継場ヶ々ヘ
飛ノ圖

ボスントン

ソウダ
フチベ
木

one station to another without the aid of a messenger." In response to naïve questions about stars and storms, Manjiro told his inquisitors that the Milky Way could be seen in other parts of the world, and that heavy rains occured almost everywhere.

Officials listened intently when this prisoner dared to disapprove of Japan's isolationist policy: "When a whale ship or a trading ship is delayed by a storm there is a shortage of water and fuel. The Japanese government drives all ships away, whether the crew is suffering or not. The Americans seek permission to get these things [at Japanese ports]."

The men endured prison for six months. Finally, in June 1852, the three were released and allowed to visit their families.

Manjiro described the telegraph to the artist who drew this picture.

*T*raveling along the Tokaido

HOME AT LAST

THEY SAILED TO THEIR HOME PROVINCE, TOSA, and hiked to Usa, where Denzo and his brother Goemon looked forward to reuniting with their mother and father. When they arrived, they were devastated. Both parents had died! The family hut had rotted into a pile of rubble. The grief-stricken brothers gratefully accepted an aunt's offer to have them live with her. It was a heartbreaking homecoming.

A depressed Manjiro set out for his own home, fearful that he, too, might be shaken by tragedy. He spent four days hiking ninety miles to his birthplace, Nakahama. He traveled along the Eastern Sea Route, the famous Tokaido, the most-traveled road in Japan. It snaked along the beautiful Pacific coast, where, in many places, mountains met the ocean. Although a major highway that started at the capital city of Edo (Tokyo), it was very narrow and rutted. Commoners went by foot. Samurai and lords traveled on horseback or sat in *kagos*, small open or enclosed platforms with poles attached that rested on the shoulders of two or four servants.

On the evening of October 5, 1852, Manjiro reached home. It had been almost twelve years since he had last seen his village, when he was fourteen years old. His mother, brothers, and sisters were startled and then elated when he entered their

hut. They were ecstatic, for they had been sure Manjiro had died at sea. Together, they visited the local temple to offer thanks for Manjiro's miraculous return—and to show him a tombstone that had been erected in his memory. In the evening, villagers gave a party to celebrate the survival of their lost fisher boy.

Manjiro was dismayed because he was allowed to be home only three days. Lord Yamanouchi, the daimyo of Tosa, wanted to see him immediately and summoned him to leave his family and report to the grand castle in Kochi. Manjiro had become a sought-after celebrity not only because of his experiences overseas but also because of his knowledge.

Lord Yamanouchi was so impressed by Manjiro's outstanding intelligence that he elevated him from the low caste of a fisherman to the high rank of a samurai—a change of status unheard of at that time. As a samurai, Manjiro was given two beautiful swords to carry at his side. And a marriage with Tetsu, the seventeen-year-old daughter of a samurai, was arranged for him through a noble go-between. He was allowed to adopt a last name—a privilege reserved exclusively for the higher classes of society. He chose Nakahama, his hometown, as a last name. Manjiro Nakahama was in charge of teaching world history, geography, and elementary English to other samurai.

As it turned out, his teaching career would be abruptly stopped by a national crisis.

Manjiro was interrogated at this castle in Kochi.

As a samurai, Manjiro carried two swords and dressed in this fashion.

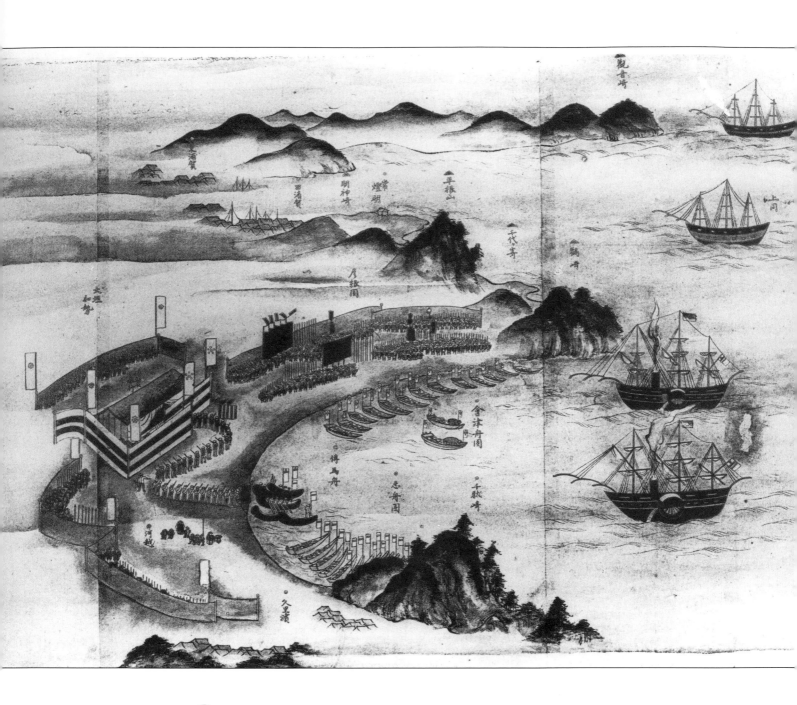

Commodore Perry's first landing in Japan on July 14, 1853,
six days after he dropped anchor in Edo Bay

HONORED SAMURAI

ON JULY 8, 1853, NINE MONTHS AFTER MANJIRO REACHED HIS HOME, a fleet of four ships of the United States Navy dropped anchor at Edo Bay. The shogun was so disturbed by this that he declared a state of emergency. Troops that had never fought wars were mobilized to combat "one hundred thousand devils." Messengers raced throughout the land to tell about "the black ships of the evil men" and to warn everyone that "hairy barbarians" might overrun the country. People panicked.

The uproar was caused by Commodore Matthew Perry, who had been sent by U.S. president Millard Fillmore with a letter asking the emperor to open Japan's ports to American ships. Although Japanese officials boarded Perry's ship with orders for him to go away, Commodore Perry refused to leave. He demanded an audience with the emperor.

Manjiro was the only man in Japan with firsthand knowledge of the United States. Therefore, he seemed best qualified to give advice. The shogun commanded him to come to Edo at once so that he could act as adviser to the Council of Nobles.

Manjiro left Kochi Castle in August 1853. He was transported by boat to the port city of Osaka, then traveled to Edo on the Tokaido Road. During this time,

Commodore Matthew Calbraith Perry

Commodore Perry's fleet had sailed away to Hong Kong to obtain more supplies—and more black warships. On February 13, 1854, the commodore returned to Edo Bay with nine heavily armed vessels. He let it be known that he intended to march to the Imperial Palace and "in the event of war he would have fifty ships in nearby waters."

Members of the Council of Nobles realized Japan's military power was weak. All their country could muster against an enemy were old weapons such as swords, pikes, antique cannons, and rusty muskets. Yet they feared that signing a treaty would mean the collapse of their government. They turned to Manjiro for advice.

Manjiro argued for an end to the nation's isolationist laws. He told the Council of Nobles that Japan could no longer lock itself away from the rest of the world; that to survive as an independent nation, Japan must peacefully agree to open ports and trade with the United States.

His opinions were welcomed by some but condemned by others. Lord Abe, who headed the council, was sure that Manjiro favored American interests. He pointed out that "Manjiro was not only saved from death by Americans but also owes a debt of gratitude for the benefits he received from them. . . . He will never act against them. Therefore [he] . . . should be not be allowed to meet the Americans."

Indeed, Manjiro was not permitted to meet the Americans. However, he played a vital behind-

A Japanese artist's portrait of Commodore Perry

the-scenes role. His translations, explanations, and comments about American documents influenced officials who were negotiating treaty terms. Manjiro described Americans as "a vigorous, capable and warmhearted people." Declaring that "it has been a long cherished desire on the part of America to establish friendly relations," he forewarned, "There are hardly any foreign weapons that can frighten Americans out of their wits."

These arguments in favor of welcoming Americans to Japan had a serious impact on the noblemen who negotiated and signed a Treaty of Peace and Amity with the United States on March 31, 1854. The treaty declared "Peace and friendship between the United States of America and the Empire of Japan." It specified that two ports, Shimoda and Hakodate, would be open to American ships. The Japanese agreed to provide Yankee whalers, warships, and merchant vessels with food, water, coal, and other needed supplies. Japan was unlocked, forced to join the modern world, after having been frozen in feudalism for two and a half centuries.

Manjiro's role as consultant continued after the treaty was signed, for Japanese leaders realized that their country needed Western technology and knowledge of other countries to survive as an independent nation. They learned about many countries. In addition to his extended stays in Hawaii and the United States, Manjiro had circled the globe on whaleboats that stopped for supplies at many places, including the French Society Islands, Spanish Guam, the Dutch East Indies, and British South Africa. He had seen foreign military installations and could describe steamships, railroads, telegraphs, and other Western scientific advances.

The Honorable Samurai Manjiro Nakahama helped bring Japan into the modern world. He designed ships capable of crossing oceans. (Laws against building big boats were no longer enforced.) As chief professor of navigation and ship engineering at Tokyo's Naval Training School, he used his own Japanese translation of the American sailing book *The Practical Navigator* as his students' textbook. He also wrote the first English book for Japanese people: *A Short Cut to the English Conversation*.

A meeting of the Japanese and the Americans was sketched by
William Speiden, Jr., one of Commodore Perry's officers.

American ships were monstrous to the Japanese before Manjiro helped
people understand their power and importance.

In 1859, Manjiro was transferred to Hakodate, in northern Japan, so that he could establish a profitable whaling industry. Manjiro used Western advanced technology to build typical New England whale ships and whaleboats. This enabled his countrymen to capture more whales than had ever been possible before. Manjiro taught them to profit from the oil and bones—valuable before petroleum and plastics replaced these products.

In 1860, he joined the first Japanese embassy to the United States as an interpreter, but his role was expanded when the ship *Karin-Maru* hit the high seas. A fierce storm sent massive waves across the deck. Captain Katsu, who had never sailed on a rough ocean, was too seasick to give commands. He handed the helm to Manjiro, who took charge. Even after the storm subsided, and until the ship reached San Francisco, Manjiro was responsible for safe sailing. When the ship returned to Japan some weeks later, the emperor awarded him with his own family Nakahama crest. It was embossed on two magnificent silk outfits.

In 1870, as interpreter for a diplomatic delegation that stopped in New York, Manjiro took two days off to travel by train to Fairhaven so that he could visit Captain Whitfield. He had not seen his American foster father for twenty-one years. Manjiro repeated in person the sentiment he had expressed in a letter he had once written to the captain. It read, "O captain how can I forget your kindness, when can I pay for your fatherly treatment? THANK GOD ten thousand times and never will forget your name."

After working as interpreter for an international conference in London, Manjiro returned to Japan and resumed teaching as a professor of English at a college that eventually became the University of Tokyo. He died in 1898 at the age of seventy-one.

Manjiro Nakahama led an incredible life in both the United States and Japan. He was indeed a citizen of both countries, and the clothes he adopted expressed this. He sponsored and symbolized a firm friendship between Japan and the United States. He could often be seen on the streets of Tokyo wearing a Japanese kimono with an American derby hat and Western shoes. To this day people still marvel at the true tale of Manjiro, the poor fisher boy who became an honored samurai.

AUTHOR'S NOTE

I BECAME FASCINATED BY MANJIRO when I learned about him during research for *Commodore Perry in the Land of the Shogun*. After years of replaying his incredible adventures in my mind, I felt impelled to write about him.

Instead of accounts of landmark events and world-famous leaders, here is the story of a poor fisher boy who became a famous samurai, a rescued castaway who became the first Japanese person to live in the United States. Manjiro subsequently worked on New England whale ships, then risked his life when he returned to Japan as an outcast.

My research was enriching. I was enthralled not only by studying Manjiro's life, but also by books about albatross, whales, whaling, American history, Japan's history, and Japanese wood-block prints. I hope to convey my enthusiasm for research to all who read this book.

Manjiro's story is well known in Japan. His tale has come to light here in the United States through the efforts of the Manjiro Society of International Exchange, in Virginia, and as a result of the Manjiro Festival, held every two years in Fairhaven, Massachusetts. Fairhaven has mapped out the Manjiro Trail so that visitors can view the homes the young castaway occupied and the schools he attended. Fairhaven and New Bedford have joined to declare themselves the sister city of Tosashimizu, part of which was, once upon a time, the poor fishing village where Manjiro was born.

His life reveals much about the social and political climate of Japan and the United States during the mid-nineteenth century. Manjiro's ordeals, adventures, and accomplishments seem sensational, melodramatic, and fictional, but they are true.

I used the following sources for information:

Bernard, Donald R. *The Life and Times of John Manjiro.* New York: McGraw-Hill, 1992.

Kaneko Hiskazu. *The Man Who Discovered America.* Boston: Houghton Mifflin, 1956.

Shoryo Kawada. *Drifting to the Southeast.* Japan: Toso Shimizu City.

Smith, Bradford. *Americans from Japan.* Philadelphia: Lippincott, 1948.

Warinner, Emily. *Voyager to Destiny.* Indianapolis: Bobbs-Merrill, 1956.

Yonekura Isamju. "Information Given at Nagasaki Trials." *East Magazine* (January 1956).

———. "Manjiro: the Remarkable Life of a Fisherman's Son." *East Magazine* (May, June 1976).

I read these books to learn about whaling:

Davis, William. *Nimrod of the Seas.* Boston: Charles E. Larueat, 1926.

Ellis, Richard. *Men and Whales.* New York: Knopf, 1991.

Melville, Herman. *Moby Dick.* New York: Penguin, 1992.

Website

Readers interested in learning more about Manjiro and his American home of Fairhaven may want to check out the John Manjiro home page, located at the following website address: *www.ultranet.com/~clongwor/*

Illustrations are reproduced courtesy of the following: page 13, American Museum of Natural History; pages 17 and 62, The Art Institute of Chicago, Clarence Buckingham Collection; pages 23 and 76, Asahi Shinbun; page 56, The Bancroft Library, University of California, Berkeley; pages 34 and 36, Bishop Museum; page 73, The Chrysler Museum, Norfolk, Virginia; pages 28, 29, and 30, Davis private collection; page 18, Heibonsha Press; pages 22, 40, 46, and 48, Kendall Whaling Museum; pages 33, 55, 64, and 65, Kochi City Public Library (Japan); pages 1 and 43, Kochi Prefectural Museum of History; page 68, The Kochi Shinbun; pages 16, 72, and 75, Library of Congress; page 8, The Metropolitan Museum of Art, The H. O. Havemeyer Collection, bequest of Mrs. H. O. Havemeyer, 1929 (29.100.507); page 14, The Metropolitan Museum of Art, bequest of Henry L. Phillips, 1939 (JP 2968); page 69, The Metropolitan Museum of Art, The Henry L. Phillips Collection, bequest of Henry L. Phillips, 1940 (JP 2905); page 80, The Metropolitan Museum of Art, The Henry L. Phillips Collection, bequest of Henry L. Phillips, 1939 (JP 2972); page 66, The Metropolitan Museum of Art, Rogers Fund, 1922 (JP 1325); page 6, The Metropolitan Museum of Art, gift of Mr. and Mrs. Harry Rubin, 1972 (1972.213 [26]); pages 4, 10, 12, 20, 26, 38, 42, 44, and 50, Millicent Library of Fairhaven, Massachusetts; page 70, Mr. Mikio Mortimatsu, president, Kokusai Micro Shashin Kogyo Sha; page 52, The Museums at Stony Brook, gift of Mr. and Mrs. Ward Melville; page 24, New Bedford Whaling Museum; page 27, Shelburne Museum; page 54, Wells Fargo; page 58, author's private collection.

ABOUT THE ILLUSTRATIONS

The sketches on pages 4, 10, 33, and 43, signed John Mung, were made by Manjiro. The illustrations on pages 44, 55, 64, and 65, which have been credited to Manjiro, are the work of artists who were reputedly guided by sketches and descriptions provided to them by Manjiro.

I could not resist including wood-block prints and other pieces of nineteenth-century art that reveal scenes of nineteenth-century Japan through artists' eyes, such as the *Great Wave off the Coast of Kanagowa* (pictured above).

ABOUT THE AUTHOR

Rhoda Blumberg "shines in the imaginative use of extensive research to tell, compellingly and entertainingly, stories from history," says *School Library Journal.*

She has written about such landmark events as the opening of Japan (1853–1854) in *Commodore Perry in the Land of the Shogun,* a Newbery Honor Book, which also won the *Boston Globe/Horn Book* Award and the Golden Kite Award; *The Incredible Journey of Lewis and Clark,* a Golden Kite Award winner; *The Great American Gold Rush,* which won the John and Patricia Beatty Award given by the California Library Association; and *The Remarkable Voyages of Captain Cook,* all ALA Notable Books. She has also covered the Louisiana Purchase in *What's the Deal?* and the development of the transcontinental railroad in *Full Steam Ahead.*

Rhoda Blumberg and her husband, Gerald, live in Yorktown Heights, New York.